W9-BAG-301

Ultimate Cars

THUNDERBIRD

Sheila Rivera

ABDO
& Daughters

VISIT US AT
WWW.ABDOPUB.COM

Published by ABDO Publishing Company, 4940 Viking Drive, Suite 622, Edina, Minnesota 55435. Copyright ©2004 by Abdo Consulting Group, Inc. International copyrights reserved in all countries. No part of this book may be reproduced in any form without written permission from the publisher.

Printed in the United States.

Edited by: Melanie A. Howard
Contributing Editor: Alan Pierce
Interior Production and Design: Terry Dunham Incorporated
Cover Design: Mighty Media
Photos: Corbis, Ron Kimball Photography, Ford Motor Company

Library of Congress Cataloging-in-Publication Data

Rivera, Sheila, 1970-
    Thunderbird / Sheila Rivera.
      p. cm. -- (Ultimate Cars)
    Summary: Surveys the history of the popular Ford Thunderbird sports car, from its first model in 1955 to its re-introduction in 2002.
    Includes bibliographical references and index.
    ISBN 1-59197-583-2
    1. Thunderbird automobile--History--Juvenile literature. [1. Thunderbird automobile--History.] I. Title. II. Series.

TL215.T46R579 2004
629.222'2--dc22
                                                                        2003060486

Contents

In Good Company 4

The Legend Takes Flight 6

The Classics 8

Ford Adds More Seats 10

The Space Racer 12

Flair Birds and Glamour Birds . . .14

Big and Small 18

Aerodynamics 20

Super Birds 22

Thunderbird Racing 24

The Modern Bird 26

Timeline 28

Glossary 30

Internet Sites 31

Index 32

In Good Company

Thunderbird. Even the name sounds powerful. Since 1955, this great American car has been flying down the highway. It was one of the first sports cars ever made in the United States after World War II.

This amazing car has seen many changes over the years. The Thunderbird's size has varied greatly. Additional comfort and safety features have been added with each new model. Over the years, the look of the car has changed dramatically. But despite all the changes, the Thunderbird is one of the most recognized cars in the American automobile industry.

Ford Motor Company was around long before it began producing the Thunderbird. The company's vehicles were among the first cars built in the United States. It all started with a young engineer named Henry Ford.

In 1899, Ford decided that he wanted to start his own automobile business. On his first try, he and several partners started the Detroit Automobile Company. But it broke up after only one year.

Ford found new investors in 1901, and started another company. But Ford wanted to build racecars. The investors disliked this idea. So, they paid Ford to leave the company, and began making Cadillacs.

But Ford was not discouraged. In 1902, he formed a partnership with Alex Malcomson. Together they created the Ford Motor Company.

The first car they made was the Model A, which came on the market in 1903. It looked like other cars of the time, but had a more powerful engine. Later, Ford went on to build the Model T. It was one of his most famous cars.

While producing the Model T, Ford started using the assembly line. The first assembly lines were used in meatpacking plants in the 1900s to speed up production. Ford started using one in his factory in 1913. He was the first person ever to use an assembly line to make cars.

The assembly line revolutionized the auto industry. Suddenly, it was possible to make cars quickly. Quick production kept the price of Ford's cars low, so more people could afford to buy them. With more cars being sold, Ford's business grew.

Today, the Ford Motor Company is one of the largest auto manufacturers in the world. It has designed and created many different car models with a variety of names. But few of its cars are as well known as the Thunderbird.

Henry Ford

The Legend Takes Flight

In 1952, Ford Motor Company stylist Frank Hershey learned that Chevrolet was making a sports car called the Corvette. Hershey had once worked under the Corvette's designer, Harley Earl. Thinking that it would be fun to show up his old boss, Hershey started working on a possible sports car design.

That same year, Ford division manager Louis Crusoe and designer George Walker visited Paris, France. They walked through Paris's Grand Palais auto salon and saw many European sports cars. Crusoe admired them.

Suddenly, Crusoe pointed at one, and asked Walker why Ford couldn't make cars like those. Walker thought quickly. Then he told his boss a fib. He told Crusoe that Ford was already making that kind of a car.

Later, Walker called the Ford plant in the United States. He asked its design team to begin working on a car like the ones Crusoe had seen in Paris. By the time the two returned to the United States, what Walker had said was true. Ford was working on its first sports car.

The two-door, two-seat convertible roadster was completed by late 1954. It was fully equipped with a 198 horsepower V-8 engine. The car had a sporty look, but it was designed to be a comfortable luxury car. This was different than its rival, the Corvette, which was built to be fast. Ford wanted its new car to be bought by people who wanted comfort instead of speed.

Even though the car was ready for production, it still didn't have a name. The Ford advertising team thought of about five thousand names, including "Beaver" and "Hep Cat." None of the names fit the car. So Ford decided to have a contest.

Ford asked its employees to come up with a name. The person who came up with the winning name would receive a new suit worth $250. That would be the same as an $800-$1,000 suit today.

Company designer Alden "Gib" Giberson offered the name Thunderbird. The thunderbird is a magical bird of Native American legend. Crusoe liked the name, and the car became the Thunderbird. Some car enthusiasts have shortened the name to T-Bird.

The 1955 Thunderbird was designed to be comfortable and sporty. The public's demand for the car surpassed Ford's expectations.

The Classics

On October 22, 1954, the first Thunderbird came off of Ford's Dearborn plant assembly line. There were 4,000 orders for the car on its first day of production. Ford had thought it would sell 10,000 1955 Thunderbirds. But sales totaled more than 16,000.

The 1955 Thunderbird was available in Thunderbird Blue, Raven Black, Snowshoe White, Goldenrod Yellow, or Torch Red. The car's interior was vinyl, and came in colors that matched the exterior paint.

Also, the car had side windows that rolled up and down. This was something that the popular Chevrolet Corvette's windows could not do.

Ford offered two options for the Thunderbird's top. Consumers could buy the car with a hardtop or a soft top. The soft top was easy to operate and the hardtop was removable. The hardtop car sold for $2,695, and the soft-top car sold for $2,765.

The next year brought many changes to the Thunderbird. Ford added porthole windows on the sides of the top for better visibility. The rear bumper was extended, and the spare tire was mounted on the back of the car.

Ford also gave the 1956 Thunderbird a more powerful engine. A 260 hp engine replaced the old 198 hp engine.

This and other features made the 1956 Thunderbird more expensive. The 1956 hardtop sold for $2,944, and the soft top sold for $3,019. With optional features, the price could run as high as $3,800.

A new grille, bumper styling, and flared tailfins were just some of the changes to the 1957 model. The Thunderbird also gained a Volumatic radio. Its controls automatically made the radio's volume go up as the car's speed increased.

Dial-O-Matic seats with memory were another interesting feature in the 1957 Thunderbird. When the engine was turned off, the seats moved back for easier entry and exit. After the engine was turned back on, the seats were programmed to move back into their set position.

Most 1957 Thunderbirds came equipped with a 300 hp engine. Racing and supercharged engines were also available.

The 1955-1957 models are the most cherished Thunderbirds by many car enthusiasts. These are the Thunderbirds people are referring to when they talk about "the classics."

Ford Adds More Seats

By the time the 1958 Thunderbird was being designed, Louis Crusoe had moved on to a higher position at Ford. Robert McNamara had replaced him as division manager. McNamara decided that the 1958 Thunderbird was going to be a four-passenger car.

Frank Hershey didn't like McNamara's plan. He quit his job so that he wouldn't have to make the new car. So George Walker designed the 1958 Thunderbird.

The 1958 model was two feet (0.61m) longer than the previous year. But it was lighter because its frame, fenders, dash, and floor were all made from a single piece of steel. The front grille and four round headlights were also new. But the 1958 model still featured the 300 hp engine.

Many Americans were pleased with the 1958 Thunderbird. They liked the added passenger room. With the car's four-seat design, whole families could enjoy the luxury of the Thunderbird.

But some people weren't happy about the extra seats. After Ford announced that they were changing the Thunderbird, a rush of orders came in for the two-seat 1957 model. In fact, there were so many requests for the 1957 model that for a while both the 1957s and 1958s were in production at the same time!

This second generation Thunderbird earned the nickname "Square Bird" because of its square roof, and angular shape. It was a great success for Ford. The Thunderbird received *Motor Trend* magazine's Car of the Year award in 1958. Sales jumped to nearly 38,000.

In 1959, the Thunderbird came equipped with a 350 hp engine. The car also had a slightly different grille and trim. This was the first Thunderbird with a fully automatic soft top. The driver could raise or lower the top by using a switch on the dash.

Ford produced more than 67,000 of the 1959 model cars. The hardtop sold for $3,696, and $3,970 bought the soft top model.

In 1960, Ford designers added a sliding sunroof to the hardtop model. There were small changes to the grille, and the side trim was removed. This made the 1960 model only slightly different than the 1959. Ford produced about 93,000 Thunderbirds that year.

The 1958 Thunderbird featured four seats instead of two. The car proved to be popular, but many Thunderbird fans preferred the sportier, two-seat Thunderbird.

The Space Racer

Ford designer Bill Boyer created a new Thunderbird design in 1961. At that time, the United States was racing with the Soviet Union to be the first country to put a man on the moon. The public was very excited about winning the Space Race. Boyer thought it would be a good idea to use that excitement to sell cars.

Boyer designed the 1961 Thunderbird to look like a rocket ship. He gave it a long, slightly pointed nose like a rocket. It had fins on the back, and the round taillights looked like a rocket's rear propulsion engines.

Standard features included power steering, power brakes, and a Cruise-O-Matic automatic transmission. The 1961 model also had a 300 hp engine. A more powerful Thunderbird Special model was also available. It had a 400 hp engine.

A swing-away steering wheel was optional in the 1961 model. This special steering wheel could swing over to the driver's right. Like the Dial-O-Matic seat introduced in 1957, this feature allowed the driver easier entry and exit. Other options included electric windshield wipers, self-adjusting brakes, and a Day-Night mirror.

The 1961 Thunderbird dazzled the public. People started calling the car the "Round Bird" or "Bullet Bird" for its rounded design. A Bullet Bird was chosen as a pace car for the

1961 Indianapolis 500 auto race. Ford continued to make the car for another two years.

Ford added two new models to the Thunderbird line in 1962. They were the Landau Hardtop, and the Sports Roadster.

The Roadster was a convertible. Designer Bud Kaufman created a fiberglass tonneau cover to hide the back seat. This gave the car a sportier look. The cover could be removed to seat four passengers.

Model prices ranged from $4,321 for the standard hardtop to $5,349 for the Sports Roadster. Ford sold more than 78,000 Thunderbirds that year.

Ford decided to make a Special Limited Edition Thunderbird Landau in 1963. It was named the Principality of Monaco Thunderbird. But many people called it the Princess Grace because Ford gave the very first one to Princess Grace of Monaco.

The Princess Grace had a white exterior with a white vinyl top. Its interior was white leather with rosewood trim. The car also had an imitation gold nameplate on the dashboard to display the car's serial number.

Only 2,000 of the limited edition Princess Grace Landaus were made. They sold for $4,748 each. Ford made more than 63,000 Thunderbirds in 1963, including the Princess Grace Landaus.

In 1962, Ford made a Thunderbird convertible.

Flair Birds and Glamour Birds

Ford introduced the "Flair Birds" in 1964. The Flair Bird was different than the Bullet Birds before it. Ford redesigned the interior of the car to have a more space-age style. The usual round taillights were replaced with rectangular lights. A longer hood made the car's shape less rounded.

People bought almost 30,000 more Thunderbirds in 1964 than in 1963. The standard hardtop sold for $4,486, the Landau sold for $4,589, and the soft top sold for $4,853. More than 92,400 Thunderbirds were made in 1964.

The 1965 Flair Birds were the first Thunderbirds to have power front disc brakes. A reversed scoop was also added behind the front wheels. Emberglo paint was available on the Special Landau Ford made that year. The Special Landau also had wheel covers, and an interior that matched the paint. It sold for $4,695.

A single taillight replaced the two rectangular taillights on the back of the 1966 Thunderbird. It also had a larger, 7.0-liter engine. This was available for people who wanted more power than the standard 6.4-liter engine could provide.

Because of these new features, the 1966 Thunderbird became a favorite among collectors. The hardtop sold for $4,395, the new Town Hardtop sold for $4,451, and the new Town Landau sold for $4,552. The soft top sold for $4,845.

The 1966 Ford Thunderbird Town Landau

Bill Boyer and David Ash restyled the Thunderbird in 1967. This was the start of a new generation of Thunderbird called Glamour Birds. The 1967 Thunderbird had hidden headlights, and the car looked both larger and lower than the previous year's model.

But the biggest change was to the doors. For the first time, the Thunderbird was offered as a four-door vehicle. The four-door Landau had suicide-style back doors. This type of door is hinged at the back, and opens at the front. The four-door Landau could comfortably carry six passengers.

With the four-door Landau, a two-door hardtop model, and a two-door Landau available, Ford had a very successful year. The company produced almost 8,000 more cars in 1967 than it had the year before. The hardtop sold for $4,603, and the two-door

The 1967 Thunderbird Landau four-door with suicide-style doors.

Landau sold for $4,704. The four-door Landau sold for $4,825. It sold for $4,924 in 1968.

A sunroof became available in 1969. The Thunderbird also went back to having two taillights instead of one. Between the taillights, Ford put a Thunderbird emblem.

The 1970 and 1971 Glamour Birds were changed slightly, but they didn't sell well. Ford gave the Glamour Birds a V-shaped grill, and a longer front end. The public didn't like the cars. Between 1970 and 1971, production dropped by more than 14,000 cars.

A view of three Thunderbird cars

Big and Small

Poor sales prompted Ford to revise the Thunderbird's design. In 1972, Ford decided to go back to making two-door Thunderbirds. It also dropped the standard hardtop, which meant that only one Thunderbird model would be sold. This was the first time since 1957 that only one model was available.

The 1972-1976 models became known as "Big Birds." They were made as two-door hardtop luxury cars. But even though the Big Birds were two-door cars, they were still longer than the Flair Birds. This was because Ford built the Big Birds on the same platform as the Lincoln Continental Mark IV.

Ford sold the 1972 Thunderbirds for $5,293. That year, Ford produced the one-millionth Thunderbird. It had custom gold paint, and a bronze medallion on the hardtop and on the dashboard.

The last year for the Big Birds was 1976. A gas shortage was making people buy more fuel-efficient cars. Thunderbirds were just too big to compete. Ford sold the cars for $7,790, then started redesigning the Thunderbird once again.

"Fashion Birds" emerged in 1977, and were produced until 1979. They had a slimmer body, and hidden headlights. Thunderbird sales were the highest to date in 1977, when Ford produced 318,000 cars.

In 1978, production jumped to almost 352,000. Ford celebrated its seventy-fifth anniversary that year by making a special Diamond Jubilee Thunderbird. This model came with a Diamond Blue Metallic or Ember Metallic exterior. Its steering wheel and dashboard were covered in leather, and it had a 22-karat gold nameplate. It sold for $10,106.

Continued demand for fuel-efficient cars made Ford change the Thunderbird again in 1980. Thunderbirds of the early 1980s became smaller and more angular than the Thunderbirds of the 1970s. They became known as "Box Birds," and were marketed for their fuel economy.

Box Birds were built on the Fox-chassis platform. They shrank to 200.4 inches (509 cm) in length. Ford made a Silver Anniversary Edition Thunderbird with special paint and trim in 1980. The two years after that, Ford produced the Heritage Editions. More than 286,000 Thunderbirds were sold by the end of 1982. That was the Box Bird's last year.

The 1978 Ford Diamond Jubilee Thunderbird

Aerodynamics

Management changed at Ford in the late 1970s and early 1980s. The new head of the Ford Design Center was Jack Telnack. Telnack had been trained in Europe. Because of this, he had a different idea about what made a good car.

Telnack looked over the designs for all of the 1983 Ford models, and hated their boxy design. He brought together the design team, and asked them what they thought the new cars should look like.

It took a while for the design team to take him seriously. At that time, designers were used to having their supervisor tell them what to make. But after the designers realized that they could make something they liked, they grew excited. The designers started over on many of the cars they'd been working on. One of them was the Thunderbird.

The 1983 Thunderbird became a coupe. Its body was completely reshaped so that it was more aerodynamic, which was how it earned the nickname "Aero Bird." It also had a 3.8-liter engine. A 2.3-liter turbocharged engine was available in the Thunderbird Turbo Coupe Ford also introduced that year. It had a five-speed manual transmission.

Ford continued to experiment with the Thunderbird's design in the 1980s. Special models that Ford produced between 1983 and 1988 included the Fila Coupe, the Elan Coupe, the Sport Coupe, and the LX Coupe. And, the 1987 Thunderbird Turbo Coupe won *Motor Trend*'s Car of the Year award.

The Turbo Coupe model revived excitement about the Thunderbird. Ford made Thunderbird Turbo Coupes from 1983 to 1988. Below is a 1986 Thunderbird Turbo Coupe.

Super Birds

The Thunderbird won *Motor Trend*'s Car of the Year Award again in 1989. This was the year that Ford began producing the "Super Birds." They remained in production until the Thunderbird's retirement in 1997.

Super Birds were the first Thunderbirds to have independent rear suspension. They were also wider, which made the back seat roomier. Super Birds also had some body styling changes that made them even more aerodynamic than the Aero Birds.

A special body restyling was done for Thunderbird's thirty-fifth anniversary in 1990. Like the 1975 and 1980 models, it received special paint and trim. This model came in black with blue striping. It also had an optional titanium lower body for contrast.

But even with all these improvements, sales slumped. Between 1993 and 1997, production dropped by almost 56,000 cars. In 1997, Ford Motor Company decided to stop making the Thunderbird.

The 1989 Thunderbird Super Coupe

Thunderbird Racing

Thunderbird racing started as early as 1955. But the first time a Thunderbird officially arrived on a track was during the Daytona Spring Speed Week in 1957. The car reached speeds of nearly 140 miles per hour (225.41 km/h) at the trials. Later that year, it reached 160 mph (257.49 km/h) at the Bonneville speed trials.

In 1959, Thunderbirds entered the National Association for Stock Car Auto Racing (NASCAR). That year it won six races, all in the top division.

The Thunderbird again made history at NASCAR in 1982. It won more than 150 races in the top division. This included four victories at the Daytona 500.

Ford Thunderbird driver "Million Dollar" Bill Elliott won 11 NASCAR events in 1985. He reached speeds of nearly 187 mph (301 km/h). Elliot won the NASCAR Winston Cup Championship in 1988. This same honor went to Alan Kulwicki in 1992.

Thunderbirds were retired from the racetrack in November, 1997. The Ford Taurus replaced the Thunderbird on the racetrack in 1998. Many racecar fans were sad to see the Thunderbird go after such a successful run.

Bill Elliot races a Thunderbird at Daytona Beach, Florida, in 1987. Thunderbird cars amassed a distinguished record at the track in the 1980s and 1990s.

The Modern Bird

In 1999, Ford unveiled a Thunderbird concept car at the North American International Auto Show in Detroit, Michigan. It was bright yellow and sleek. And like other new cars of the time, it had a retro look. People loved it, and Ford started producing the cars for the 2002 model year.

The Modern Bird enchanted the automotive world. It had some of the same design features as earlier Thunderbird classics. These included an egg-crate grille, round headlights and taillights, and porthole windows on the hardtop.

It also came with many safety and luxury features. They included standard anti-lock disc brakes, and an optional all-speed traction control system to improve stability. It had a V-8, 252 hp engine. The 2002 Thunderbird sold for $35,945 and up, depending on options.

The Thunderbird was chosen as the official pace car at the Rolex 24 at Daytona, and at the Grand American Road Racing series in 2002. It also received the People's Choice Car of the Year award as well as *Motor Trend*'s Car of the Year award. The Thunderbird has won *Motor Trend*'s Car of the Year award more times than any other car model.

Horsepower was increased to 280 for the 2003 Thunderbird. It had a V-8 engine, and a five-speed automatic transmission.

Standard safety features included dual airbags, all-speed traction control, and power anti-lock disc brakes on all four wheels.

Desert Sky Blue and Mountain Shadow Gray were the new colors available for the 2003 model. The car also featured leather interior, automatic temperature control, and a six-disc CD player. The 2003 Thunderbird convertible with a soft top sold for $37,420. The convertible with a removable top sold for $39,915.

A limited edition 2003 Thunderbird was featured in the James Bond film *Die Another Day*. The 007 Thunderbird had a coral exterior with a white removable top, white leather seats, and chrome wheels. Only 700 of these cars were produced. The 007 Thunderbird sold for $43,995.

New collectors colors for the 2004 Thunderbird were Merlot, and Vintage Mint Green. Also, a Light Sand interior became available. The 2004 Thunderbird convertible retailed for $37,650 for the Deluxe model, and $38,695 for the Premium model. With added features, the 2004 Thunderbird could cost more than $42,000.

Ford has future plans to retire the Thunderbird again. But for loyal Thunderbird lovers, this is a car that will never die. The Thunderbird is an American icon. It will never be forgotten.

Timeline

1901

Henry Ford and Alex Malcomson form a partnership to start Ford Motor Company.

1913

Ford Starts using the assembly line to make cars.

1952

Frank Hershey, Louis Crusoe, and George Walker get the idea to have Ford Motor Company make a sports car.

1954

First Thunderbird rolls off the Dearborn plant's assembly line.

1958

Ford Motor Company makes the Thunderbird as a four-seat car. This model wins *Motor Trend*'s Car of the Year award.

1959

The Thunderbird joins NASCAR. It wins six top division races.

1967

The Thunderbird becomes a four-door car.

1972

Ford Motor Company goes back to a two-door Thunderbird model. The one-millionth Thunderbird is produced.

1978

Ford Motor Company celebrates its seventy-fifth anniversary with the Diamond Jubilee Thunderbird.

1980
The Thunderbird celebrates its silver anniversary.

1982
The Thunderbird wins more than 150 NASCAR races in the top division.

1983
The Thunderbird becomes a coupe, and goes to a new aerodynamic shape.

1987
The Thunderbird wins *Motor Trend*'s Car of the Year award.

1988
"Million Dollar" Bill Elliot wins the NASCAR Winston Cup with his Thunderbird.

1989
The Thunderbird wins *Motor Trend*'s Car of the Year award.

1992
Alan Kulwicki wins the NASCAR Winston Cup driving his Thunderbird.

1997
Ford Motor Company stops making the Thunderbird. It is also retired from the racetrack.

1999
Ford unveils a Thunderbird concept car at the North American International Auto Show in Detroit.

2002
The first modern Thunderbird goes on the market.

Glossary

convertible: a car with a top that can be removed. It can have a soft top or a hardtop.

coupe: a car with a permanent top.

fiberglass: a durable, nonflammable material that is made from fine threads of glass.

grille: a metal grating on the front of a car.

horsepower: a unit of measure originally equal to the pulling strength of a horse. Modern horsepower measurement is equal to 746 watts.

pace car: a high-performance car that leads a group of competing racecars through a pace lap of a race. The pace car does not participate in the race.

porthole: a small circular window.

rear propulsion engine: the engine on a rocket or space shuttle.

roadster: an open automobile with a single seat, capable of accommodating two to three passengers, and a rumble seat or luggage compartment in back.

technology: the use of scientific knowledge to practical problems.

transmission: a group of gears and parts which transmit power from a car's engine to a driving axle.

V-8: a V-type engine has two rows of cylinders set at a 60 to 90 degree angle to one another, and a single crankshaft running through the point of the V. A V-8 engine has eight cylinders.

Internet Sites

www.abdopub.com

Would you like to learn more about the Thunderbird? Please visit **www.abdopub.com** to find up-to-date Web site links about the Thunderbird and other Ultimate Cars. These links are routinely monitored and updated to provide the most current information available.

Index

007 Thunderbird 27

B

Bond, James 27
Bonneville 24
Boyer, Bill 12, 16
Box Birds 19
Bullet Bird 12, 14

C

Cadillac Automobile Company
    4
Crusoe, Louis 6, 7, 10

D

Daytona Spring Speed Week 24,
    26
Dearborn, Michigan 8
Detroit Automobile Company 4
Detroit, Michigan 26
Die Another Day 27

E

Elliott, Bill 25

F

Flair Birds 14, 15, 18
Ford, Henry 4, 5

G

Glamour Birds 16
Grand American Road Racing
    Series 26

H

Hershey, Frank Q. 6, 10

I

Indianapolis 500 13

K

Kaufman, Bud 13
Kulwicki, Alan 25

L

Landau Hardtop 13–16
Lincoln Continental 18

M

McNamara, Robert 10
Monaco 13
Motor Trend 11, 21, 22, 26

N

NASCAR 24, 25
North American International
    Auto Show 26

P

Princess Grace 13

R

Rolex 24 at Daytona 26
Round Bird 12

S

Special Limited Edition 13
Sports Roadster 13
Square Bird 11
Super Birds 22

T

Thunderbird Special 12
Turbo Coupe 20, 21

W

Walker, George 6, 10